TOP DAWGS

Celebrating a championship season for the Georgia Bulldogs

Book design by **Josh Crutchmer**

Photos courtesy of AP Images

© **2022 KCI Sports Publishing**

ISBN: 978-1-957005-06-5

Printed in the United States of America

CONTENTS

Top Daws

Georgia Bulldogs – National Champions!

Sounds pretty good doesn't it? Georgia fans have waited 41 long years to utter those words, and now, the Bulldogs are back on top.

Let the celebration begin!

This was a championship 12 months in the making. After two heartbreaking losses to Alabama and Florida kept the Bulldogs out of the 2020 college football playoffs, Coach Kirby Smart and the returning Georgia players headed into the offseason with one goal in mind—winning a national championship in 2021.

Led by one of the most dominating defenses in college football history, Georgia opened the year with a huge win over perennial national power Clemson and then proceeded to roll through the SEC regular season. With an explosive offense adept at rising to the occasion this Georgia team will go down as one of the greatest in the school's storied history.

In the following pages enjoy a trip down memory lane of this incredible championship season that came to its jubilant conclusion with the National Championship game victory in Indianapolis over SEC rival Alabama.

Georgia fans cheer at Sanford Stadium during a win over Alabama-Birmingham in September.

At last!

Georgia turns in a fourth quarter for the ages en route to national title

NDIANAPOLIS — Stetson Bennett delivered the biggest throws of his storybook career, and Georgia's defense sealed the sweetest victory in program history, vanquishing rival Alabama 33-18 in the College Football Playoff championship game for its first national title in 41 years.

Bennett connected with Adonai Mitchell on a 40-yard touchdown to give No. 3 Georgia a 19-18 lead with 8 minutes, 9 seconds left and then hooked up with Brock Bowers for a 15-yard score on a screen to put the Bulldogs up eight with with 3:33 left.

The final blow came from Georgia's dominant defense. Kelee Ringo intercepted an underthrown deep ball down the sideline by Heisman Trophy winner Bryce Young. Instead of going down with a little more than a minute left, Ringo took off and behind a convoy of blockers and went 79 yards for a touchdown that set off a wild celebration by the Georgia fans who packed Lucas Oil Stadium.

The Bulldogs (14-1) hadn't won a national title since freshman Herschel Walker led them there in 1980. If simply snapping the drought wasn't good enough, doing against No. 1 Alabama (13-2) had to make it feel even better.

Nick Saban's Crimson Tide had won seven straight against the Bulldogs, including the last four against Georgia coach Kirby Smart, Saban's longtime assistant.

Bennett, the former walk-on turned starter, finished 17-for-26 for 224 yards and no interceptions.

For most of the first three quarters, first CFP title game to be a rematch of a regular-season game was an old-fashion Southeastern Conference defensive struggle.

The first touchdown of the game came with 1:20 left in the third quarter. After James Cook broke a 67-yard run to get the Bulldogs into the red zone, three more running plays — and a face-mask

Georgia's coach Kirby Smart kisses the trophy after a 33-18 national championship win over Alabama.

penalty by Alabama — got them into the end zone. Zamir White went in standing up from a yard out with massive defensive tackles Jalen Carter and Jordan Davis leading the way as blockers. The Bulldogs led for the first time at 13-9.

After Alabama added another field goal, the Tide caught a break on a strange turnover by the Bulldogs.

As Bennett was being taken down deep in Georgia territory, he tried to throw the ball away. The ball slipped loose and bounced toward the sideline, seemingly harmlessly. Alabama's Drew Sanders casually caught the ball as he was jogging out of bounds.

Surprisingly, the ruling on the field was a fumble recovered by the Tide, and replay upheld the call, giving the Tide the ball in the red zone. A few plays later, Young eluded the rush and found Cameron Latu for a 3-yard touchdown that put Alabama up 18-13 with 10:14 left in the fourth.

It felt again that Georgia would not be able to break whatever spell Alabama seemingly had on the Bulldogs.

Bennett was 13-for-22 for 141 yards as the next drive started, and you practically could hear all skeptical Georgia fans wondering why Smart didn't turn to his four-star backup QB, J.T. Daniels, for a spark.

As he has done so many times during a career that started on the scout team and took a detour through junior college in Mississippi, the small-town Georgia kid nicknamed "Mailman" came through.

Bennett completed all three of his passes for 68 yards, including a long strike to Mitchell for a touchdown with 8:09 left that gave the Bulldogs a 19-18 lead after a failed 2-point conversion.

The Georgia defense clamped down on Young, forcing a three-and-out on the Tide's next drive, and then Georgia went to work on sealing a long-awaited championship.

Georgia's Adonai Mitchel catches a touchdown pass over Alabama's Khyree Jackson to give the Bulldogs a 19-18 lead in the fourth quarter of the national championship game.

Kelee Ringo returns an interception for a touchdown to seal a 33-18 win over Alabama.

The Georgia defense blocks a crucial second-half field goal attempt by Alabama's Will Reichard.

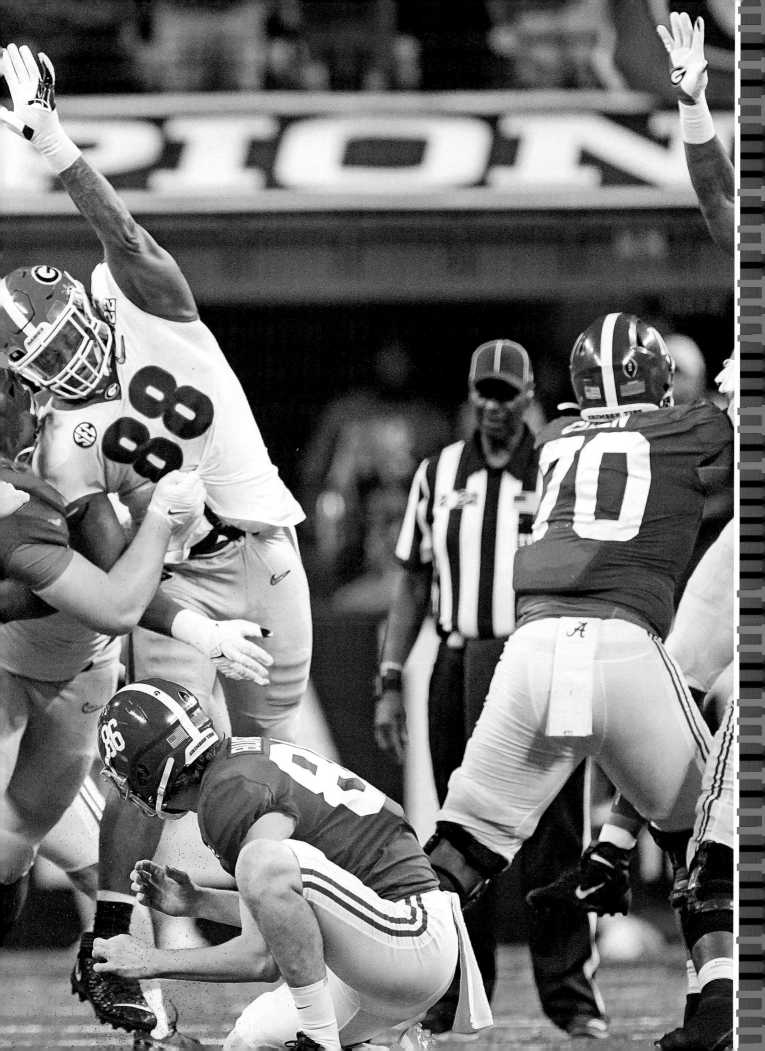

Georgia's Christopher Smith stops Alabama's Ja'Corey Brooks on a first-half rushing attempt.

Brock Bowers runs into the end zone to finish a 15-yard scoring pass from Stetson Bennett that put the Bulldogs up 26-18 in the fourth quarter.

Georgia's Zamir White celebrates after scoring the Bulldogs' first touchdown of the national championship game.

Bulldogs linebacker Nakobe Dean pursues UAB Blazers running back Jermaine Brown Jr.

Defensive gem

Georgia stymies third-ranked Clemson to open in style

CHARLOTTE, N.C. — Georgia coach Kirby Smart knew his defense was super athletic.

He didn't know they would be this good.

Christopher Smith returned an interception 74 yards for a touchdown and the fifth-ranked Bulldogs turned in a defensive effort for the ages, toppling No. 3 Clemson 10-3 in the opener for both teams.

The Bulldogs held the Tigers to 2 yards rushing and sacked D.J. Uiagalelei seven times to position themselves for a serious run at the College Football Playoffs.

"You find out a lot more about yourself when you play in these kinds of games," the Bulldogs coach said following the impressive defensive performance.

Uiagalelei finished 19 of 37 for 178 yards with one interception. He bobbled snaps, was out of sync with his receivers and spent most of the day under heavy duress against a relentless Bulldogs pass rush.

"We frustrated and confused them," Smart said.

No offensive touchdowns were scored in a game matching two of the best defensive lines in college football, but that lack of big plays from the offense didn't dampen the feeling for quarterback JT Daniels.

"Do I have a half bad feeling?" asked Daniels. "Hell, no. We just beat Clemson. I'm happy."

Even when Georgia turned the ball over, the Tigers couldn't take advantage.

Trailing 7-0 in the third quarter, Baylon Specter appeared to give the Tigers some momentum when he intercepted JT Daniels' pass at the Georgia 33. But after a short gain on first down Uiagalelei was sacked on consecutive plays and Clemson was forced to punt.

Clemson didn't score until 9:08 left in the game when a 44-yard reception by Joseph Ngata and a

Bulldogs linebacker Channing Tindall celebrates a tackle for a loss late in a 10-3 win over Clemson.

defensive pass interference penalty set up a 22-yard field goal by B.T. Potter, helping the Tigers avoid their first shutout since 2003.

Despite being dominated all game, the Tigers had a chance to tie with 7:35 left when they took over at their own 25. Clemson reached midfield and Dabo Swinney went for on fourth-and-5, only to see Uiagalelei's hurried pass fall incomplete. From there, the Bulldogs ran out the clock.

"I knew we were would be pretty good and pretty deep on defense," Smart said. "But we're more athletic than when we were in the past."

The loss leaves Clemson with a razor-thin margin for error when it comes to making its seventh straight College Football Playoff appearance. No team has ever made the playoff with two losses since the new four-team format began in 2015.

"I'm not going to write the season off because we lost 10-3 to a top five team," Swinney said.

Georgia's defense, which dominated the line of scrimmage, set the tone early with Nolan Smith and Nakobe Dean registering third-down sacks on Clemson's first two possessions.

The only touchdown of the game came late in the second quarter when Smith jumped in front of a Uiagalelei pass intended for Justyn Ross and raced 74 yards to the end zone to give the Bulldogs a 7-0 lead at halftime. Swinney placed the blame on Ross making a bad decision on the route, saying he was supposed to "sit down or turn out" but instead kept running a slant.

"That's the receiver putting the quarterback in bad spot," Swinney said. "He just didn't make the right decision."

Uiagalelei wasn't blaming anyone but himself.

"I didn't play well today and everyone could see that," Uiagalelei said.

"The important thing is we've got to get better," Smart said. " What I did find out is we've got a lot of resilience and when our offense had to convert and force the ball down the throat of a pretty good defense, we were able to do it. That makes me proud."

Georgia running back Kendall Milton leaps past Clemson cornerback Malcolm Greene in the second half.

Bulldogs linebacker Nolan Smith sacks Tigers quarterback D.J. Uiagalelei in the first quarter.

Georgia quarterback JT Daniels takes a snap in the third quarter as the Bank of America Stadium crowd looks on.

Super sub

Backup Stetson Bennett throws five touchdowns as Dawgs roll

ATHENS, Ga. — Stetson Bennett did his best to create a quarterback controversy at Georgia.

Stepping in for injured starter JT Daniels, Bennett tied a school record with five touchdown passes in the first half to lead No. 2 Georgia to a 56-7 rout of UAB.

The senior completed his first five passes - four of them going all the way to the end zone for the Bulldogs (2-0), who didn't show any signs of a letdown after a 10-3 victory over Clemson in the opener.

Bennett, a former walk-on, started five games last season before Daniels claimed the job.

It looks as if Bennett hasn't given up on winning it back.

"I guess it's just an innate confidence," he said. "If you believe you're good enough, it really doesn't matter the situation that is thrust upon you."

Jermaine Burton set the tone by slipping behind the secondary to haul in a 73-yard TD from Bennett on Georgia's second offensive play, thrilling the raucous crowd of nearly 93,000 at Sanford Stadium.

It was the first full house between the hedges since the 2019 season. Crowds were limited to about 20,000 last season because of the pandemic.

By the opening minute of the second quarter, Bennett had scoring passes of 12 yards to Kenny McIntosh, 89 yards to Brock Bowers and 61 yards to Arian Smith.

At that point, Bennett's passer rating was a staggering 775.6. The Blazers' secondary didn't put up much resistance, leaving Burton, Bowers and Smith wide open with blown coverages.

"It always helps when you've got great players all over the field," Bennett said.

Bennett tacked on his fifth TD pass of the game with another to Bowers, the freshman tight end finding a seam in the zone to grab a 9-yard throw that sent the Bulldogs to the locker room with a 35-0 halftime lead.

Bennett played only one more series in the second half and, yes, led the Bulldogs to another TD. He set it up with a 20-yard scramble - Georgia's longest run of the day - before James Cook took it in from the 14.

Bennett finished 10 of 12 passing for 288 yards and became the sixth Georgia quarterback to pass for five touchdowns in a game. The most recent was Aaron Murray vs. New Mexico State in 2011.

"He's always had great composure, great athletic ability and a great understanding of the game,"

Georgia wide receiver Arian Smith celebrates a first-half touchdown with Adonai Mitchell against UAB.

coach Kirby Smart said. "He's meant a lot to this program. All he does is do his job each and every day."

Daniels was sidelined by an oblique injury, which is not believed to be a long-term problem. He was in uniform on the sideline, but the Bulldogs had no reason to risk a more serious issue by playing him against a team that was a 25 1/2-point underdog.

Once Daniels was ruled out, Smart made a bit of a surprising call on the starter. Redshirt freshman Carson Beck was listed as No. 2 on the depth chart, but the Bulldogs went with the more experienced signal-caller.

Great call.

While some fans groaned when Bennett was introduced as the starter, remembering his up-and-down results in 2020, there were nothing but cheers after he lit up the Blazers (1-1).

Georgia scored touchdowns on six of seven possessions with Bennett in the game.

So, what's the quarterback situation going forward?

"It depends on JT's injury, it depends on how we practice during the week," Smart said. "It's a day-to-day evaluation. I don't get into hypotheticals."

The Bulldogs' defense wasn't too shabby, either. The unit has yet to allow a touchdown this season while scoring two itself, following up a pick-six against Clemson with another on Jamon Dumas-Johnson's 21-yard interception return for a score.

UAB was held to 174 yards overall on a miserable day for quarterback Tyler Johnston III, who completed just 6 of 14 for 39 yards with three interceptions.

"Give Georgia all the credit. They are super talented," UAB coach Bill Clark said. "They have a great defense and their special teams are unreal. There is no doubt that they are deserving of that No. 2 ranking."

The Blazers avoided a shutout when Keondre Swoopes picked off a pass from Beck and returned it 61 yards for a score.

Jermaine Burton catches a pass from Stetson Bennett for a touchdown on the opening drive against UAB.

Bulldogs linebacker Nakobe Dean pursues UAB Blazers running back Jermaine Brown Jr.

No debate needed

Daniels returns, defense dominant in win over South Carolina

THENS, Ga. — So much for any debate about Georgia's starting quarterback.

JT Daniels has a firm grasp on the job.

Daniels returned from injury with three touchdown passes, backing up another stellar performance by Georgia's defense that carried the No. 2 Bulldogs to a 40-13 victory over South Carolina.

Daniels completed 23 of 31 for 303 yards, including scoring throws of 43 yards to Jermaine Burton, 38 yards to freshman Adonai Mitchell and 4 yards to James Cook.

"I definitely felt very confident," said Daniels, who missed the previous game with an oblique injury.

Georgia (3-0, 1-0 Southeastern Conference) finally gave up a touchdown while on defense when Luke Doty, getting the ball on the Bulldogs' side of the field after a fumble, connected with Josh Vann on a 36-yard touchdown pass with 10:55 remaining.

"Of course, that upsets us," said Georgia linebacker Nolan Smith, who had a huge night. "When we say no one in the end zone, that's what we mean."

With Doty playing for the first time this season, South Carolina (2-1, 0-1) gave up three sacks and a safety, along with two turnovers that led to Georgia touchdowns.

But the offense could take some satisfaction from being the first to score a touchdown on the Bulldogs. Until then, the only TD against Georgia had come on an interception return.

Daniels sat out a 56-7 victory over UAB, watching as backup Stetson Bennett tied a school record with five touchdown passes.

Daniels wasted no time re-establishing his hold on the No. 1 spot, completing a 21-yard pass to Brock Bowers on his very first snap and guiding

Coach Kirby Smart leads the
Bulldogs out of the tunnel before
their 40-13 win over South Carolina.

the Bulldogs to the end zone on their first two possessions.

"Only one of us can play, and everybody is dying to be that guy," Daniels said. "Everybody in the room wants to play every game."

Bennett got a shot the third time the Bulldogs had the ball. He promptly threw an interception that was returned to the Georgia 12, setting up a field goal.

Daniels returned to the game and didn't leave until early in the fourth quarter with the outcome no longer in doubt.

"We let the coach make the decision on who's going to play and when," Daniels said. "I'm happy when Stetson plays great and he's happy when I play great."

After punting the ball away in the closing seconds of the first half and content to settle for a 21-6 lead, Georgia wound up scoring five more points.

Backed up on their own 1, the Gamecocks explicably attempted to throw out of the end zone. Doty was sacked by Jordan Davis and Smith for a safety.

Then, after receiving the free kick, Daniels completed three passes for 39 yards to set up Jack Podlesny's 36-yard field goal as time expired, sending Georgia to the locker room up 26-6.

Georgia put it away in opening minute of the second half, again sparked by a huge defensive play.

Doty's pass was picked off by Derion Kendrick, who returned it to the South Carolina 20 to set up Zamir White's 5-yard touchdown run.

"They're not doing anything special on defense. They're just really good," said South Carolina's Shane Beamer, who took his first loss as a head coach. "They line up and say, 'We're better than you. Come beat us.'"

JT Daniels throws a first-half touchdown pass as South Carolina defensive end Jordan Strachan pressures him.

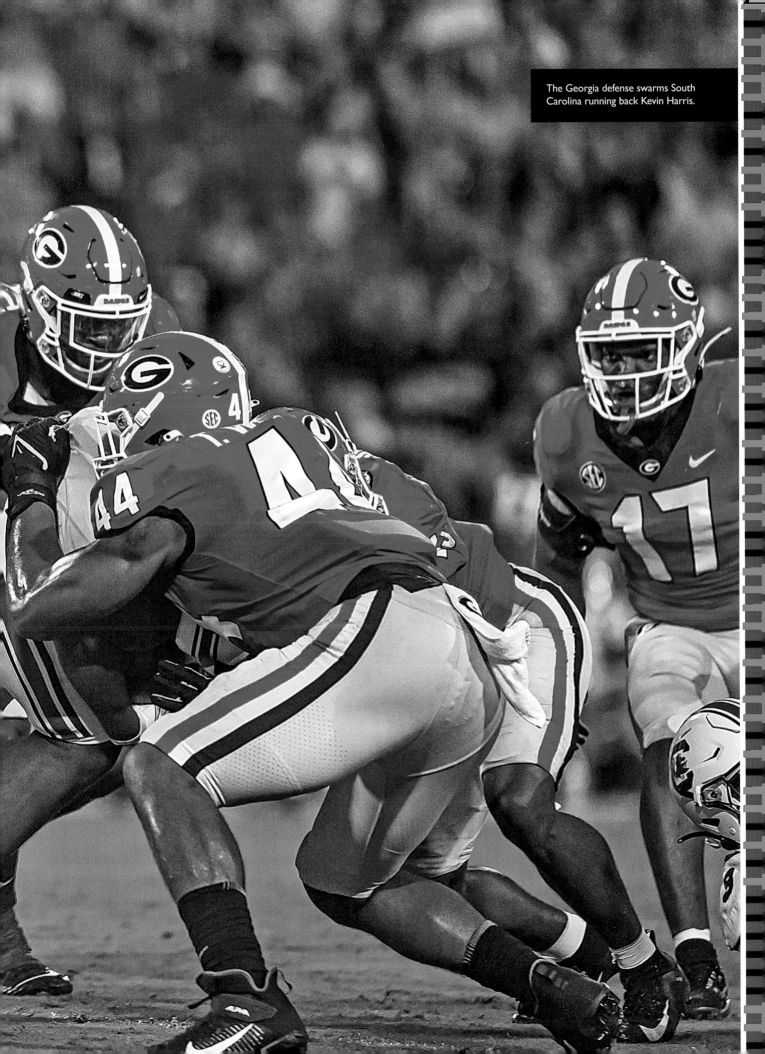

The Georgia defense swarms South Carolina running back Kevin Harris.

No contest

Starter Daniels plays one quarter, Dawgs shut out Commodores

NASHVILLE, Tenn. — Georgia coach Kirby Smart spent the week talking about Mike Tyson, pushing his Bulldogs to start fast and play up to the standard he wants this season.

His Bulldogs did just that.

JT Daniels threw for 121 yards and two touchdowns playing only the first quarter as No. 2 Georgia dominated Vanderbilt 62-0 in the Bulldogs' biggest win in a series that started in 1893.

This game was effectively over when Georgia (4-0, 2-0 Southeastern Conference) led 35-0 after the first quarter. The Bulldogs started three of four drives in Vandy territory. They recovered a fumble on a kickoff to set up one TD, then Christopher Smith intercepted a pass to set up a second TD less than 30 seconds later.

"You got to be elite all the time," Smart said. "You can't be some of the time. It's not how elite teams play, and our guys embrace that and I was proud of them."

Bulldogs' fans turned this into their home away from Sanford Stadium in what Smart called an "incredible" turnout with Georgia red even in seats behind the Vanderbilt bench. They got to watch the Bulldogs post their first shutout this season, forcing Vandy three-and-out nine times.

Georgia nearly had more points than Vandy managed yards, outgaining the Commodores 524-77 no matter how deep Smart substituted.

"We say nobody in our end zone," Georgia linebacker Nolan Smith said. "That's the standard, that follows for everybody."

Vanderbilt (1-3, 0-1) lost its fourth straight to Georgia and its 14th straight SEC game, a skid that could be longer if COVID issues hadn't forced Vandy to cancel its visit on Georgia's Senior Day last season. A program that won in Athens in 2016 showed how much rebuilding first-year coach Clark Lea faces.

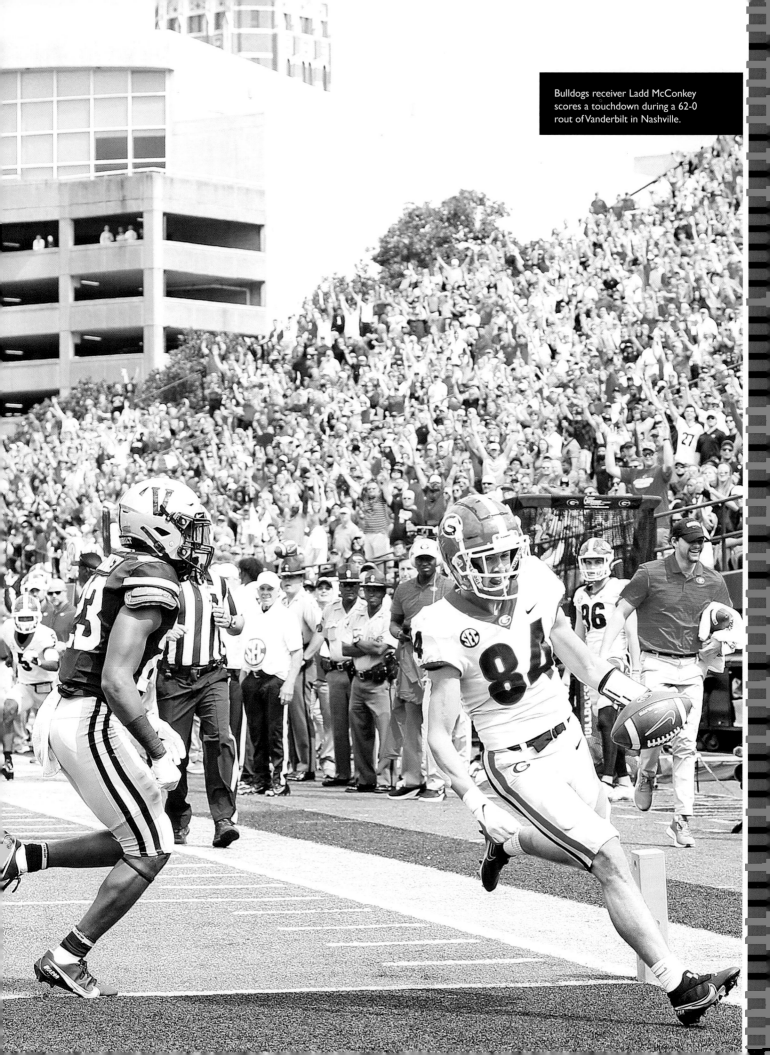

Bulldogs receiver Ladd McConkey scores a touchdown during a 62-0 rout of Vanderbilt in Nashville.

"We came out flat, we turned the ball over, we made mistakes especially in the special teams area," Lea said. "And look. It doesn't matter who you play against. You're setting yourself up for disappointment. For me, this isn't about them. It's about us. It's about how we perform."

Tight end Brock Bowers started the scoring with a 12-yard run on an end around with 11:21 left, and he became the first Bulldogs' player to run for a TD and catch a TD pass in the same game since Todd Gurley did it against Florida in 2013. Bowers later caught a 29-yard pass from Bennett in the third quarter.

Ladd McConkey, the redshirt freshman receiver, hauled in a 12-yard touchdown pass from Daniels for his first score as a Bulldog.

McConkey (4 catches for 62 yards) soon added his second going from his slot position to take a handoff and go around the left side for a 24-yard touchdown run.

"We've been working on it in practice," McConkey said. "It made it easy for me. The downfield blocking made it easy for me."

Smart said that perimeter blocking keyed the scores, crediting Jermaine Burton on the Bowers TD run and Justin Robinson on the McConkey scoring run.

"End arounds are misdirection plays," Smart said. "They complement our run game. "

Smart pulled Daniels, who is now 7-0 as a starter, after the first quarter. Stetson Bennett threw for 151 yards and a TD himself.

"It was a situation we felt like we could get Stetson some reps, and things kept rolling," Smart said of the early substitution at quarterback.

Ladd McConkey runs past Vanderbilt safety Dashaun Jerkins.

Georgia defensive back Dan Jackson (47) jumps on Georgia Bulldogs defensive lineman Jalen Carter to celebrate a stop against Vanderbilt.

Another test passed

White runs wild as Georgia cruises over Arkansas

THENS, Ga. — Georgia's determination to win its top-10 matchup against Arkansas on the ground had nothing to do with which quarterback started for the Bulldogs.

Instead, it was all about taking what the Arkansas defense gave Georgia — and the Bulldogs just kept taking and taking. And that made it even easier for the Georgia defense to dominate.

Zamir White rushed for two touchdowns and recovered a blocked punt for another score, and No. 2 Georgia pounded No. 8 Arkansas 37-0 in the Bulldogs' second consecutive shutout.

Georgia (5-0, 3-0 Southeastern Conference) raced to a 21-0 lead in the first quarter despite playing without quarterback JT Daniels, who was held out with a right lat injury.

Stetson Bennett filled in for Daniels and passed for only 72 yards as the Bulldogs relied on their running game and top-rated defense to beat

Arkansas (4-1, 1-1).

"They were basically challenging us, could we run the ball," Bennett said. "They said we couldn't but we said we could today."

The Bulldogs rushed for 273 yards and wore down the Arkansas defense, holding the ball for 36 minutes.

The matchup of top-10 SEC teams turned into a statement game for Georgia.

"I think we know how good we are," Bennett said. "I think we know what it takes to be that good every week."

Georgia, leading the nation in total defense and scoring defense after last week's 62-0 win at Vanderbilt, held Arkansas to 10 first downs and 156 yards. Linebacker Nakobe Dean and defensive tackle Devonte Wyatt each had 1 1/2 sacks.

The last time Georgia recorded back-to-back shutouts in SEC games was in 1980, its last national championship season.

Georgia running back Zamir White breaks through the Arkansas line on a second-half touchdown run.

"Every time we get on the field, we are pushing for a three and out," Dean, a junior linebacker, said. "That is just the standard. If they do not score, they cannot win. We just try to do our job and get them off the field and get the offense the ball."

Georgia coach Kirby Smart said he understood the significance of the consecutive conference shutouts.

"It's 1980 rare," Smart said. Of course, all Bulldogs fans know 1980 was the last time Georgia won the national championship.

"We were patient today but aggressive, and that's hard to beat," Smart said. "We preached that all week — one series at a time, not getting ahead of ourselves. I felt like Arkansas had a really good team, but that if we were patient while still being aggressive and physical that we could at least impose some of our own will."

It was a sobering experience for Arkansas second-year coach Sam Pittman, the former Georgia offensive line coach.

"I don't want to simplify this, but they just whipped us physically," Pittman said. "We couldn't block them and we couldn't get off blocks for much of the day."

Georgia stuck to the run as Arkansas aligned its defense with extra defensive backs.

Georgia stretched its lead to 21-0 when walk-on defensive back Dan Jackson blocked Reid Bauer's punt and White fell on the ball in the end zone.

Arkansas also had quarterback questions after KJ Jefferson missed most of the second half of last week's win over Texas A&M with a bruised left knee. Jefferson completed 8 of 13 passes for 65 yards. Malik Hornsby replaced Jefferson in the final quarter.

Jack Podlesny kicked field goals of 46, 30 and 37 yards. Cam Little was wide right from 37 yards in the second quarter for the Razorbacks.

Running back Kendall Milton and lineman Jamaree Salyer (69) celebrate a touchdown for Georgia in the second half.

Georgia defensive back Dan Jackson blocks the punt in the endzone by Arkansas's Reid Bauer in the first quarter. The Bulldogs recovered for a touchdown.

Order maintained

Bennett once again heeds call, stands out in rout of Tigers

AUBURN, Ala. — Stetson Bennett and No. 2 Georgia's defense were more than enough to take care of Auburn yet again.

Bennett passed for 231 yards and two touchdowns and led the Bulldogs past No. 18 Auburn for the second straight year in a 34-10 victory Saturday even if the defense did allow an opponent to reach the end zone for a change.

The nation's top defense gave up only its second touchdown of the year for the Bulldogs (6-0, 4-0 Southeastern Conference), who were still without injured starting quarterback JT Daniels. None of that kept Georgia from another comfortable SEC win and a fifth straight in the Deep South's Oldest Rivalry.

"What a tough environment to play in," said Georgia head coach Kirby Smart. "I give a lot of credit to Auburn and their fans. They created an electric environment. For a lot of our players,

probably over 50 percent or more, they have never played in a road environment. Two of our DNA traits are composure and toughness, and I thought that has never been more evident than it was today. Composure and toughness. The men in that locker room never doubted and never questioned each other."

Bennett, who made his first college start in a Top 10 matchup with Auburn (3-2, 1-1) last season, completed 14 of 21 passes and hit Ladd McConkey in stride for a 60-yard third quarter score. He also had a 30-yard run.

Daniels is out with a lat injury for the second straight week, along with some sidelined receivers.

"It's next man up mentality," Smart said. "That's what we talked about all week. We've got a lot of guys hurt and beat up, including the quarterback. We feel like he's getting better, but Stetson played a heck of a game."

But the Jordan-Hare Stadium crowd didn't

Georgia quarterback Stetson Bennett inadvertently strikes a popular pose on a first-half run against Auburn.

seem to bother the Bulldogs, who dominated in the trenches on both sides.

"Any time you come over here and play this team it's a war," said Bennett. "I think our offensive line and defensive line won the battle at the line of scrimmage. It was so much fun. I had a blast."

Zamir White ran for 79 yards on 18 carries with two touchdowns, doing most of his damage in the second half.

Bo Nix and the Tigers came in averaging 40 points per game but couldn't solve the Georgia defensive puzzle despite moving the ball at times. Nix completed 21 of 38 passes for 217 yards with an interception off a dropped ball a week after delivering a comeback win at LSU.

Georgia also sacked Nix four times and harried him all afternoon, and the Tigers had some other drops to boot. The Bulldogs allowed just 46 yards on 29 rushes.

"We've got to finish drives," Auburn coach Bryan Harsin said. "That's the most frustrating thing right now. We can drive the field and that really doesn't matter if you don't put points on the board."

Auburn had failed fourth-down passes end its final drive of the first half and its opening one in the second. Nix griped about what he thought was a missed call on the first one intended for Ze'Vian Capers.

"The guy completely grabs him. I thought it should have definitely been a pass interference," he said. "Obviously if it had been them they probably would have called it, but that's just part of the game, part of the rivalry."

Bulldogs running back James Cook hurdles an Auburn defender.

Georgia running back Kendall Milton carries the ball between Auburn safety Bydarrius Knighten and linebacker Chandler Wooten.

Another statement

Georgia defense takes points personally against upstart Kentucky

ATHENS, Ga. — The final seconds were meaningless.

Except to the Georgia defense.

For the first time all season, the fearsome Bulldogs gave up two touchdowns in a game. It didn't really matter as they romped to another victory — their first as the nation's new No. 1 team — with a 30-13 triumph over No. 11 Kentucky.

Still, their desire to keep Kentucky from scoring at the end, and the lengths the Wildcats went to for their second TD, epitomized where Georgia's at right now.

The Bulldogs (7-0, 5-0 Southeastern Conference) aren't content just to win.

They want to bury opponents.

"There may only be 4 seconds left in the fourth quarter, but we still don't want anybody in our end zone," linebacker Adam Anderson said. "I'm still hurting right now."

Stetson Bennett, starting his third straight game in place of injured JT Daniels, threw for 250 yards and three touchdown passes — two of them to freshman tight end Brock Bowers.

With the game decided, Kentucky (6-1, 4-1) drove to a first down at the Georgia 1 in the final minute.

Will Levis was stuffed on a quarterback sneak. JuTahn McClain was stopped for no gain. Instead of letting the clock run out, the Wildcats called their final timeout.

Finally, they scored. Levis delivered a quick slant to Wan'Dale Robinson, who dove into the end zone with 4 seconds remaining, while what was left of the crowd at Sanford Stadium booed loudly.

Georgia's defense had given up only two touchdowns all season. Kentucky managed to double that total, though the Bulldogs weren't done yet.

Clearly angry, they blocked the extra point to

Kentucky quarterback Will Levis is sacked by Georgia defensive lineman Jalen Carter (88) and linebacker Quay Walker (7) during the first half.

keep one last point off the board.

"It's just pride," said coach Kirby Smart, whose team is surrendering a miniscule 6.6 points a game. "When you're competing at the highest levels to be the best in the country, that doesn't change — regardless of the scoreboard or the time on the clock."

The Bulldogs limited Kentucky to 243 total yards, while also blocking a field-goal attempt on the final play of the third quarter.

"They're a great defense," Levis said. "I think we were able to do some things that we're going to be proud of looking at the tape, but could've had opportunities to do a little more."

Sitting at 6-0 for the first time since 1950, the Wildcats pulled out all stops, even running a hook and lateral. But they followed up 330 yards rushing in a win over LSU with a mere 51 yards on the ground against Georgia.

Leading only 14-7 at halftime, the Bulldogs took the second-half kickoff and drove 75 yards in six plays to effectively finish off the Wildcats and gain a stranglehold on the SEC East race.

An apparent 59-yard touchdown pass to Bowers was negated by a holding penalty, but Bennett connected again with the freshman in the right corner of the end zone for a 27-yard score that did stand.

Bowers had another TD on a 20-yard play with about 11 1/2 minutes remaining to make it 30-7. He finished with five receptions for 101 yards.

After a scoreless opening quarter, Georgia scored on back-to-back possessions. James Cook took a short pass 19 yards to the end zone, and Zamir White followed with a 24-yard scoring burst right up the middle.

Late in the first half, Kentucky finally got something going.

Catching a break when a video review overturned a fumble call, the Wildcats covered 75 yards in 13 plays, converting three times on third down. Levis capped it off with a 1-yard touchdown pass to Justin Rigg.

Bulldogs defensive lineman Devonte Wyatt celebrates a 30-13 victory over Kentucky.

Tight end Brock Bowers catches a touchdown pass in front of Kentucky defender J.J. Weaver during the fourth quarter.

Party won't stop

Dawgs overwhelm Florida, assert revenge for previous year's matchup

JACKSONVILLE, Fla. — Raise a glass to Georgia's defense. Or three, actually — one for each second-quarter turnover that turned the rivalry known as "The World's Largest Outdoor Cocktail Party" into another lopsided affair.

The top-ranked Bulldogs and the nation's No. 1 defense dominated Florida, scoring three touchdowns off miscues in a 12-play sequence that carried them to a 34-7 victory, their fourth in five years in the neutral-site game.

Georgia (8-0, 6-0 Southeastern Conference) later clinched the league's Eastern Division thanks to Kentucky's loss at Mississippi State.

Coach Kirby Smart's team won its 12th straight since getting steamrolled in Jacksonville a year ago. The Bulldogs' injury-riddled defense allowed 571 yards in that one, the most in Smart's six seasons.

Georgia vowed to not let it happen again and responded with another demoralizing effort that might be their most impressive all season.

"It was real personal," linebacker Nolan Smith said.

Florida (4-4, 2-4) managed no points, 11 first downs and 214 yards through three quarters and looked like its decades-old, NCAA-record scoring streak might be in jeopardy down the stretch. But the Gators finally got on the scoreboard with 2:49 remaining, extending the streak to 418 games. They have scored in every outing since getting shut out by Auburn in 1988.

Emory Jones' late touchdown run, though, did little to negate Georgia's mastery for three-plus hours on a cool, sundrenched afternoon. All the empty seats on Florida's side of TIAA Bank Field told the real story.

This one was over by halftime.

And Georgia's defense deserved a toast for making it happen.

"It was a whole bunch of momentum," Smart

Florida quarterback Anthony Richardson is tackled by Georgia defensive back Lewis Cine (16), linebacker Quay Walker (7) and defensive back Christopher Smith in the first half.

said. "You get momentum like that, it can be an over-swell."

Smith started the onslaught by ripping the ball out of Anthony Richardson's arms at the end of an 8-yard run. James Cook sliced his way through Florida's defense for a 10-yard touchdown run on the ensuing play.

Richardson was making his first career start, getting the nod over turnover-prone Jones. But he wasn't the difference Florida fans expected.

"The talent's there," Gators coach Dan Mullen said. "We've just got to get him coached up on the intangibles."

Two plays later, Travon Walker tipped Richardson's pass over the middle and Smith intercepted it. Stetson Bennett, who started his fourth consecutive game in place of JT Daniels, found Kearis Jackson for a 36-yard score on first down.

Trailing 17-0, Richardson had Florida on the move before throwing a pass that Nakobe Dean picked off and returned 50 yards for a touchdown.

"It's just momentum swings," Smith said. "Anyone could have done it. The Nakobe pick-six was a momentum swing. When momentum goes the other way, guys feed off of each other. You feel it."

Getting turnovers was the Georgia's lone weakness all season. Smart said an assistant coach ran down the statistics in the locker room and showed the unit it was in the top three in every category except turnovers; the Dawgs were 68th.

"That offends our guys," Smart said. "I can't say that's why we got turnovers. But that challenged their pride."

The Bulldogs scored three times in 2:09. The last team to score three TDs in that little time at the end of a half was Utah State, which did it in a 52-26 win over Boise State in 2015.

"There was great excitement, great energy today," Smart said. "Our fans really impacted the game. They helped us get them for a few offsides. The turnovers were the difference in the game. We had a few, too, but theirs were in their territory, and that was probably the biggest difference in the game."

Georgia running back James Cook stretches the ball across the goal line for a touchdown during the first half of a 34-7 win.

Zamir White rushes for a 42-yard touchdown past Florida cornerback Jason Marshall Jr. (3) and safety Mordecai McDaniel (32) during the second half.

Georgia players and fans are joined by coach Kirby Smart in celebration after a dominant win over Florida.

Paper Tigers

Daniels returns under center as Georgia smothers Missouri

ATHENS, Ga. — With Missouri gearing its defense to stop the run, No. 1 Georgia relied on big plays in a passing game that was boosted by the return of quarterback JT Daniels.

Stetson Bennett passed for 255 yards and two touchdowns before giving way to Daniels, the former starter, leading the Bulldogs to a 43-6 win over Missouri.

The game opened new questions for Georgia at quarterback while affirming the Bulldogs' season-long defensive dominance. Missouri was held to 273 total yards in Georgia's seventh game of the season allowing no more than 10 points.

"I think ... their game plan was not to let us run the ball," Bennett said. "They were trying to stop our run game and when they do that we have to try to be explosive."

The Bulldogs completed four passes of 31 yards or longer and seven for at least 15 yards. Wide receivers Jermaine Burton, who had a 47-yarder, and Arian Smith, who had a 35-yard scoring catch from Bennett, have returned from injuries to boost the unit's depth.

"Arian might be the fastest dude in the country playing football," Bennett said. "It was man-to-man and I trusted him to get to a spot, and he got there and finished the play off."

As usual, Georgia's defense led the way. The Bulldogs began the day leading the nation with 6.6 points allowed per game. Jamon Dumas-Johnson and Travon Walker had sacks.

Georgia (9-0, 7-0 Southeastern Conference) scored 40 straight points after Missouri's early 3-0 lead. Still, coach Kirby Smart wasn't satisfied, calling the overall performance "subpar" and noting the modest rushing total of 168 yards.

"We started out kind of sloppy today," Smart said. "A little bit of a lack of focus early, especially on defense. Offensively, it took us a while to get

Bulldogs receiver Kearis Jackson carries the ball in the open field against Missouri.

going, but once we did we really did some nice things. I was proud of the guys."

"We were trying to stop the run," Missouri coach Eliah Drinkwitz said. "... When you do that you're susceptible to the passing yards. Credit to them, they made a couple of really good plays and a couple of really good catches."

"They played the same defense they've been playing," Smart said. "They played a little better, they changed out a couple of guys personnel wise, but they didn't change their defense by any means. We didn't run the ball real well, but they did max blitz a little more and took some more chances than they normally do."

Daniels opened the season as Georgia's starter before missing more than a month with a lat injury. He came off the sideline midway through the third quarter. His 7-yard scoring pass to Ladd McConkey gave Georgia a 40-3 lead.

"We're blessed to have two quarterbacks who can go out there and both play at a high level," McConkey said.

Daniels' second possession ended with an interception by Missouri defensive back Jaylor Carlies.

Missouri (4-5, 1-4) also could have ongoing questions at quarterback.

Freshman quarterback Tyler Macon passed for 74 yards and ran for 42 in his first start. He shared time with Brady Cook, who threw for 78 yards.

"We were just trying to see if one of them could really spark us and sustain us," Drinkwitz said, adding "both of them did some really good things."

Jermaine Burton gets into the endzone past Missouri defensive back Akayleb Evans in the second half.

Missouri running back BJ Harris is stopped by the Georgia defense in the second half.

Rocky Toppled

Tennessee no problem for Dawgs, who dominate both sides of ball

KNOXVILLE — The Georgia Bulldogs are ranked No. 1 and just finished off a perfect run through the Southeastern Conference schedule.

They're not satisfied yet.

Stetson Bennett ran for a touchdown and threw for another as Georgia routed Tennessee 41-17.

The Bulldogs (10-0, 8-0, No. 1 CFP) went unbeaten in the SEC regular season for the first time since the league split into divisions in 1992 and went to an eight-game schedule.

"Nobody thinks they've arrived," Georgia coach Kirby Smart said. "There's things we can continue to work to get better at, and they'll continue to do that. But tonight? They went through a tough gauntlet in our league and played well."

Georgia already had its fourth berth in the SEC championship game in five years locked up coming into this game. The Bulldogs last went undefeated in league play in 1982 with a 6-0 mark, also the last time the Bulldogs started 10-0.

"It's been 39 years, so it's special ..." Bennett said. "We are a real talentedteam, but we respect everybody that we play. We don't think we are God's favorite team. We know that nobody is going to give us anything. We have to earn it."

The Bulldogs actually trailed by their largest margin this season after Tennessee scored a touchdown on the opening drive. Georgia also was down 10-7 at the end of the first quarter, new territory for the Bulldogs, who had only trailed by a field goal each to Auburn and Missouri.

Georgia responded by reeling off 27 straight points, including 17 in a dominating second quarter. Derion Kendrick intercepted a pass by Hendon Hooker, and Channing Tindall stripped Hooker of the ball — Tindall had three of Georgia's six sacks.

"We didn't come up here to take shots," Smart said. "We came up here to throw them."

Bennett converted the interception into a 9-yard

Georgia running back Kenny McIntosh leaps as he's hit by Tennessee linebackers Roman Harrison (30) and Jeremy Banks (33) during the second half.

TD run midway through the second, and he capped a 90-yard drive with a 23-yard TD pass to James Cook just before halftime. Cook also ran 10 times and matched his career high with 104 yards and two more TDs. Stetson finished with 213 yards passing and ran for 40 more.

Tennessee (5-5, 3-4) had five-time NFL MVP Peyton Manning, former All-Star first baseman Todd Helton and WNBA champ Candace Parker on hand along with an announced crowd of 100,074 for a team coming off a win at Kentucky, its first upset of a Top 20 team on the road since 2006.

The Vols' biggest win in this game came in with 3:38 left before lots of empty seats. Joe Milton hit Cedric Tillman on a 12-yard TD, giving Tennessee the most points scored against Georgia in a game this season.

"Me personally, just knowing how hard I am on myself and how much of a standard I hold for this defense, I'm not happy about that touchdown, Georgia linebacker Nakobe Dean said.

Tennessee came in second in the Bowl Subdivision scoring an average of 1.59 points per minute. Georgia and the stingiest scoring defense, which had allowed 6.6 points a game, simply smothered the Vols. The Bulldogs held Tennessee to 9 yards total offense in the second quarter.

"You've got to make some plays to give yourself a chance to play it to the end," first-year Tennessee coach Josh Heupel said. "Red zone wasn't good enough. Losing the turnover (battle) 2-0 hurt."

"Hats off to Tennessee," Smart said. "I think they've got a really good football team. This is a tough place to play, tough atmosphere to play in, but we had excellent focus and detail from our guys … they just continue to be resilient and fight through adversity."

Georgia linebacker Nakobe Dean tackles Tennessee quarteback Hendon Hooker in the first half of the Bulldogs' win.

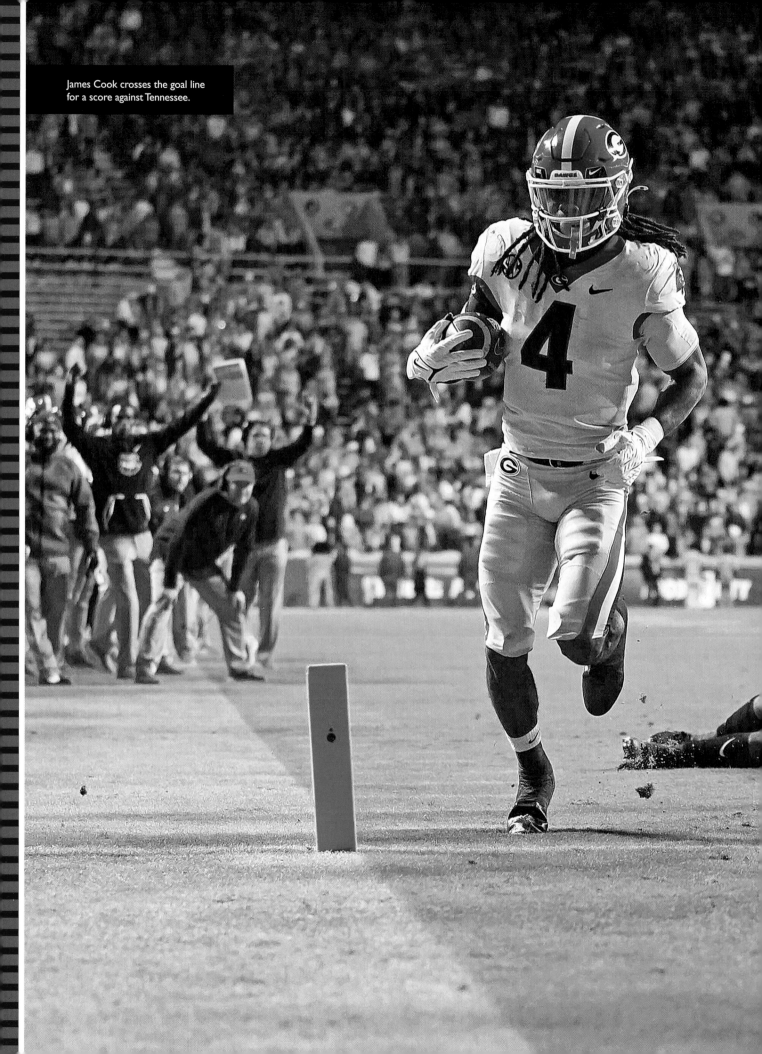

James Cook crosses the goal line for a score against Tennessee.

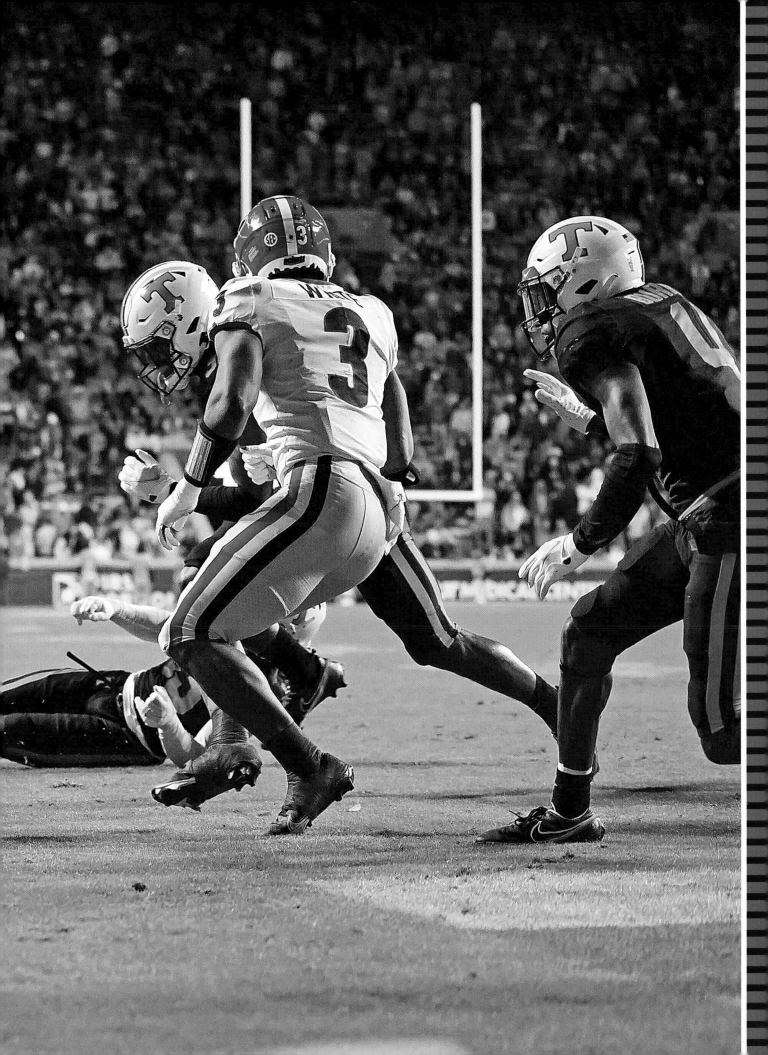

Georgia running back
James Cook celebrates a
touchdown with teammates.

Super senior

Jordan Davis scores in Georgia's final home game of season

A THENS, Ga. — As the leader of the nation's top defense, Jordan Davis has produced enough highlights to receive some Heisman Trophy hype. Davis made another memory in his farewell to Sanford Stadium.

The standout defensive tackle scored his first career touchdown and No. 1 Georgia was again dominant in a 56-7 rout of Charleston Southern on Senior Day.

Davis began the day among the seniors honored in a pregame ceremony. He ended it directing the Georgia Redcoat Marching Band. He was presented a red uniform jacket as an honorary member of the band.

"If today was not my favorite memory, I don't know what to tell you," Davis said.

Georgia (11-0) was in full control against Charleston Southern (4-6), the Football Championship Subdivision team from the Big South.

The Buccaneers fell to 0-25 all-time against FBS teams.

The Bulldogs allowed only 126 yards - 68 rushing on 31 carries and 58 passing.

"Man, tough when you are playing the No. 1 team in the country," said Charleston Southern coach Autrey Denson. "There is no room for error, so we had to play a perfect game, our best game of the season. Unfortunately, we did not do that in all phases, but man did they compete their tails off."

The Bulldogs installed a goal-line play for Davis in practice this week but there was no guarantee they would use it. As it turned out, Davis didn't have to wait very long as he scored on a 1-yard plunge out of the Bulldogs' jumbo package for the game's first touchdown.

It's not often that quarterback Stetson Bennett has the opportunity to hand the ball to a 6-foot-6, 340-pound running back.

"That was my whole job on the play, make sure

Georgia defensive lineman Jordan Davis celebrates with Bulldog fans during a win over Charleston Southern.

he gets the ball and gets the right handoff," Bennett said. "Make sure he gets in the end zone. It was pretty cool."

Davis had previously played in the jumbo package as a blocker, but fans roared in anticipation when the massive lineman shifted to the backfield. Davis was stopped on his first run from the 2. Fans again cheered when he was given a second carry and scored from the 1.

The celebration with teammates began in the end zone and continued on the sideline.

"I felt like it was just a way to honor me and send me out with a bang," Davis said. "I was excited, just knowing the team was behind me."

Brock Bowers had two touchdown catches and four Georgia players, including Davis, had scoring runs. Zamir White ran for 83 yards, including a 40-yard touchdown, on only four carries.

Bennett and JT Daniels split time at quarterback. Bennett threw scoring passes of 32 yards to Kenny McIntosh and 4 yards to Bowers.

Daniels, who began the season as the starter, took over in the second quarter and added a 7-yard touchdown pass to Bowers. Carson Beck, Georgia's third-string quarterback, took over in the second half after Georgia led 49-0 and added the Bulldogs' fourth scoring pass to tight end Brett Seither.

Georgia's defense, which recorded back-to-back shutouts over Vanderbilt and Arkansas in the first half of the season, began the day leading the nation with only 7.6 points allowed per game.

Jordan Davis, lining up as a running back, leaps into the end zone for a first-half touchdown on Senior Day at Sanford Stadium.

Georgia receiver Jaylen Johnson tries to haul in a pass against Charleston Southern.

Still state champs

Bulldogs overwhelm Tech in renewal of 'Clean Old-Fashioned Hate'

ATLANTA — Stetson Bennett helped No. 1 Georgia finish a perfect regular season, and then shifted his attention to Alabama.

Bennett passed for 255 yards and four touchdowns, including two to tight end Brock Bowers, and No. 1 Georgia overwhelmed Georgia Tech 45-0.

"It's a big accomplishment," Bennett said. "Now the real fun starts."

Georgia (12-0) gained momentum for next week's much-anticipated Southeastern Conference championship game against No. 3 Alabama in Atlanta.

In the rivalry known as "Clean Old-Fashioned Hate," the Bulldogs played a clean game with no turnovers or penalties.

"I thought our guys started fast," said Georgia head coach Kirby Smart. "We challenged them to start fast. I was pleased with no penalties. We had some sloppy series offensively and defensively, but overall, they came out and executed to a standard. They didn't play to the scoreboard, they played to our standard and I was proud of what they were able to do."

It is the first undefeated regular season for the Bulldogs since 1982, when they capped a streak of three consecutive SEC championships with tailback Herschel Walker.

Georgia now can focus on its drive for SEC and national championships.

"What we have done in the regular season is all good, but if we don't finish it the right way none of this matters," said linebacker Nakobe Dean, who led the defense with six tackles and two quarterback hurries.

Georgia Tech (3-9) finished with three wins for the third consecutive season under coach Geoff Collins, who acknowledged this week he will need to show improvement next year. The Yellow Jackets

Bulldogs tight end Brock Bowers takes off on a 77-yard touchdown reception against Georgia Tech.

closed the season with six consecutive losses following a 3-3 start.

The losing streak included losses to No. 6 Notre Dame and Georgia by a combined margin of 100-0 the last two weeks, putting more heat on Collins.

"The last two games were a step back," Collins said. "Let's get that out of the way. Against two of the top six teams in college football. But every other game, the way we've matured and closed the gap, that's real."

Georgia Tech has not closed the gap on Georgia. The battle for state bragging rights was a mismatch.

Georgia, which began the day leading the nation with its averages of 7.5 points and 236 yards allowed, posted its third shutout while giving up only 171 yards.

"I've coached a lot of seasons in the SEC," Georgia coach Kirby Smart said. "Three shutouts is hard to come by."

Bowers had a 77-yard touchdown catch, and Kenny McIntosh added a 59-yard scoring run. Bowers, a freshman, also scored on a 9-yard catch. He has 10 touchdown receptions, a school record for tight ends.

Relying on its top-ranked defense and Bennett's accurate passing, Georgia was dominant in its fourth consecutive win in the state rivalry. The Bulldogs gave up only 67 yards in the first half.

Jordan Yates made his third consecutive start, and sixth overall, at quarterback for Georgia Tech. Yates passed for only 73 yards, including a 40-yard completion to tight end Dylan Leonard in the third quarter. That drive ended with a fourth-down incompletion from the Georgia 33.

Georgia's defense delivered another fourth-down stop early in the fourth quarter. Yates fielded a low shotgun snap and was sacked by Robert Beal for a loss of 10 near midfield.

Bennett completed 14 of 20 passes, including scoring passes of 25 yards to Jermaine Burton and 11 yards to Ladd McConkey. Daijun Edwards had a 3-yard scoring run in the fourth, with quarterback JT Daniels and other backups on the field.

Georgia offensive lineman Justin Shaffer (54) and running back Kenny McIntosh celebrate with fans after a convincing win over Georgia Tech.

Jermaine Burton makes a catch for a touchdown as Georgia Tech defensive back Myles Sims defends in the first half.

Humbled

Alabama pushes Georgia defense around in SEC championship upset

ATLANTA — Georgia lost more than the SEC championship game to Alabama.

Just in time for the College Football Playoffs, No. 1 Georgia's proud defense also lost its bid to be regarded as one of the best in recent history.

The Bulldogs, who led the nation in fewest yards and points allowed this season, were exposed by quarterback Bryce Young, wide receiver Jameson Williams and No. 4 Alabama's powerful offense in a 41-24 loss.

After entering the game ranked No. 1 in the College Football Playoff, Georgia is expected to remain in the top four when the playoff field is announced.

"It didn't do any damage," coach Kirby Smart said of his team's playoff hopes. "What it did was reinvigorate our energy. ... Unfortunately, it came in a setting like this."

Georgia (12-1) had not been challenged all season. The Bulldogs' stiffest tests came in a 41-17 win at Tennessee and a 30-13 home win over Kentucky.

Left tackle Jamaree Salyer, who started after missing four games with a foot injury, said the Bulldogs can turn the loss into a positive.

"I think more than anything we've got to come together as a team," Salyer said. "It's all about how we respond. ... I feel like that wake-up call will help propel us."

When asked if he believed 12 lopsided regular-season wins had left the Bulldogs complacent, Salyer said "I wouldn't say complacency. I would say sense of urgency. ... You can always have more sense of urgency."

Halftime would have been a good spot for a renewed sense of urgency. A Georgia team which did not give up more than 17 points in a full regular-season game trailed the Crimson Tide 24-17 at the break.

Young then opened the second half with a 55-yard touchdown pass to wide receiver Jameson Williams, who had a 67-yard scoring catch earlier in the game. Williams dominated the defense with seven catches for 184 yards and two touchdowns.

Linebacker Nakobe Dean said all blame shouldn't be placed on the secondary.

"I feel like pass coverage and pass rush go hand in hand," Dean said, adding Young "being able to keep his eyes downfield" while not facing significant pressure left too much burden on the defensive backs. Georgia was held without a sack.

The Crimson Tide gained 536 yards and Young set SEC championship game records with 421 yards passing and 461 yards of total offense.

Georgia's defense led the nation by allowing only 6.9 points per game in the regular season. The

Alabama quarterback Bryce Young breaks a tackle by Georgia defensive lineman Travon Walker.

ease with which Alabama scored on five consecutive possessions cast a cloud of suspicion over the defense — and on the Bulldogs' regular-season schedule.

Salyer anticipated that criticism.

"A lot of people will say we didn't play nobody," Salyer said before adding, "The SEC is the SEC. ... I think we earned the right to be in the College Football Playoffs."

Clearly, Alabama's offense was far more powerful than any unit the Bulldogs faced in their untarnished regular season.

Any suggestion that Alabama's impressive offensive showing was a fluke could be answered quickly with this reminder: The Crimson Tide also defeated the Bulldogs by the same 41-24 score in the 2020 regular season.

The proud Georgia defense was humbled as it allowed more yards passing in the first half — a championship-game record 286 by Young — than it had in any game this season.

The Crimson Tide's yards came in large chunks, with Williams and John Metchie III consistently open.

"We had two or three third downs when we had a bust or cut a guy loose, and we hadn't done that all year," Smart said. "When you get these guys down, you've got to get off the field."

When asked what strategy he might change if Georgia plays Alabama in the playoff, Smart said, "The first answer would be don't leave people uncovered."

Turnovers also hurt Georgia. Stetson Bennett threw for 340 yards and three touchdowns, but he also threw two interceptions.

"You can't have those plays against a team like this, and they made us pay for it," Bennett said.

A bright spot for Georgia was tight end Brock Bowers, who had 10 catches for 139 yards and a touchdown.

Williams' 67-yard scoring catch for Alabama's first touchdown in the second quarter was the longest gain — run or pass — against the Bulldogs this season.

Georgia coach Kirby Smart talks to his players during the SEC championship game.

Georgia tight end Brock Bowers breaks free for a 18-yard touchdown during the fourth quarter.

Smart ball

Coach sets sights on Georgia's first national title since 1980

Kirby Smart did his best to get ahead of the questions about Nick Saban while acknowledging the topic was inevitable. It seems the Georgia coach can't avoid Saban, when championships — and Smart's big-game legacy — are on the line.

Smart is 0-4 against Saban, his former boss at Alabama. That includes Georgia's 41-24 loss to Saban's Crimson Tide in the Southeastern Conference championship game in Atlanta on Dec. 4.

The Georgia coach insisted the Georgia-Alabama rematch for the national title is not about Smart vs. Saban.

"Each game has been different," Smart said. "And it will never be about he and I. I know he won't make it that and I won't make it that, because that's for you guys to do that."

Smart's Georgia legacy is on the line. That's about more than how he compares with Saban, already assured of being remembered as one of the greatest coaches in college football history.

As Smart wraps up his sixth season at his alma mater, the national championship game will help determine his place in Georgia history. That includes how he will be judged in comparison with his predecessor, Mark Richt, as well as Vince Dooley, who won Georgia's last national championship in 1980.

Smart was hired to give Georgia the push it lacked to win the biggest games. He was hired to bring championships to the Bulldogs.

Smart, now 46, knows winning a national championship is the last step in making his program truly elite.

"If it's not coming, then what are we doing?"

Smart said before the season. "I don't look at it from the perspective of winning. I look at it from the perspective of what's important now, what are we doing now? And I know the people in this organization, the administration, the people in the state, the people that love Georgia and the energy and enthusiasm they have, it's been long overdue, right? So, for me, that's the end game, that's the goal. That's what you're always trying to work toward."

By bringing the Bulldogs to another national title game, Smart has made Georgia a regular part of the championship picture. He has brought Georgia to the biggest games.

Saban has blocked Smart's path to big-game success. Smart can change that script by winning the biggest game of all in his second national title appearance against Alabama.

Saban has won seven national championships, including six in the last 12 years at Alabama. He is looking for back-to-back titles with the Crimson Tide.

Smart was the defensive coordinator on Saban's Alabama staff before he was hired to lead Georgia's program.

Smart's Bulldogs were 12-0 following their first undefeated regular season since 1982 and on track for their first national championship in 41 years before the SEC title game loss to Alabama.

Sure, Smart doesn't deny that Saban and Alabama are a hurdle the Bulldogs have not yet cleared. Smart says he's not alone.

Smart said the Crimson Tide "have also been a problem and a thorn for any team they've played besides ours. We have that in common with a lot of teams."

Kirby Smart has a laugh with
Alabama coach Nick Saban before
the SEC championship game.

A historic sweep

Davis, Dean land national honors for world-class defense

Georgia defensive tackle Jordan Davis won the Outland Trophy as the best lineman in the nation and the Bednarik Award as the best defensive player at The Home Depot College Football Awards.

It was a historic achievement for Davis, who becomes the first SEC player in history to win both the Outland Trophy and the Bednarik Award in the same season. Nebraska's Ndamukong Suh (2009) and Pitt's Aaron Donald (2013) are the only other players to record the feat.

Davis was the only defensive player who was a finalist for the Outland Trophy, and he becomes the second Bulldogs' player to win the coveted award, joining Bill Stanfill (1968).

The 6-foot-6, 350-pound Davis is the second Georgia player to win the Bednarik, joining College Football Hall of Famer David Pollack (2004).

Not to be outdone, junior linebacker Nakobe Dean won the prestigious Butkus Award as the nation's top linebacker, joining former Bulldog and current Chicago Bear Roquan Smith as the only two winners in program history

Davis and Dean have helped Georgia lead the nation in scoring defense (9.5 points per game) and rank second in total defense (254.3 yards per game) and third nationally in rushing defense (81.7 yards per game).

Davis anchors the interior line with 28 tackles, 3.5 tackles for loss and two sacks. Dean is tied for the team lead with 61 stops, including a team-leading 8.5 tackles for loss and five sacks, and he has two interceptions and a forced fumble.

Davis and Dean are leaders on Georgia's self-annointed "No-Name Defense" which pays tribute to the team-first mentality the group plays with.

"We embrace that No-Name defense, because it's all parts working together, not just an individual thing," Davis said. "You can't have a car and not have a steering wheel to drive, or a wheel or a tire. It takes all of the parts to get that thing moving."

"Honestly this season has been so fun, (and) I'm so glad I came back," Davis said. "I couldn't have made a better decision. It's just fun. I'm enjoying the ride, having fun, every moment of it, even the part about waking up early. It's just, like, you don't have many opportunities like this.

"This is a once-in-a-lifetime experience to play for the University of Georgia, and I just want to savor it, to enjoy every moment of it."

Again, I think it's a really good start."

"My approach is always 'two on me, someone's free."

Jordan Davis

Georgia's Nakobe Dean, shown celebrating against Arkansas, won the Butkus Award as the nation's top linebacker.

Mad Dawgs

Fired-up Georgia crushes Michigan, gets Alabama rematch

IAMI GARDENS, Fla. — With one overwhelming half at the Orange Bowl, No. 3 Georgia showed that a humbling loss to Alabama did not break the Bulldogs.

In fact, it might have made them even stronger.

Stetson Bennett threw three touchdown passes, Nakobe Dean led an angry defense and Georgia returned to its dominant ways, beating No. 2 Michigan 34-11 to advance to the College Football Playoff championship.

"Answered a million questions about our team, bouncing back and how you played," Georgia coach Kirby Smart said. "We've got a lot of high-character guys on this team and they played their tail off today."

Georgia (13-1) earned a rematch with Southeastern Conference nemesis Alabama (13-1) in the title game Jan. 10 in Indianapolis.

It was 27 days ago the Crimson Tide rolled through the Bulldogs, shattering their air of invincibility after a 12-0 regular season in which they were hardly challenged.

"All our guys did was work," Smart said about how they responded to the loss and three weeks of being asked what went wrong.

The Bulldogs quickly answered any questions about whether the damage from that 41-24 setback would linger.

Georgia became the first team in the eight-year history of the CFP to score on each of its first five possessions and led 27-3 at halftime.

"We knew we were better than what we showed that last game," Bennett said.

Michigan (12-2) entered its first playoff appearance off a milestone season, having ended a long drought against rival Ohio State on the way to winning the Big Ten.

"Let'er rip," Michigan coach Jim Harbaugh told ESPN moments before kickoff.

The Bulldogs most certainly did, playing like a team out to prove a point.

Georgia scored touchdowns the first two times it had the ball, moving it at will against Heisman Trophy runner-up Aidan Hutchinson and the Michigan defense.

Bennett found freshman tight end Brock Bowers for an 8-yard touchdown pass to cap an 80-yard opening drive.

"That set the tone for the game," Smart said.

Georgia grabbed a two-touchdown lead, hitting Michigan with some of the trickery the Wolverines have used so well. Tailback Kenny McIntosh swept to the right and let loose a perfect pass to Adonai Mitchell for an 18-yard TD that made it 14-0 less than five minutes into the game.

The Wolverines had rolled to their first Big Ten championship since 2004 without trailing by as many as seven points this season.

"I mean, we gave everything we got, and we got beat tonight," quarterback Cade McNamara said. "But I think once we give it a little time, we'll be able to appreciate a lot of the great things we were able to accomplish this season."

The Bulldogs tacked on field goals on their next two possessions and Bennett connected on a 57-yard touchdown pass to Jermaine Burton streaking down the sideline to make it 27-3 with 1:38 left in the half.

And that was pretty much that. The Bulldogs outgained the Wolverines 330-101 in the first 30 minutes.

Georgia defensive back Derion Kendrick celebrates with the Orange Bowl trophy after a rout over Michigan on New Years Eve.

"I thought our (defensive) front controlled the line of scrimmage. I thought our offensive line controlled the line of scrimmage," Smart said. "That's a total team effort."

The Georgia defense that was setting an historic pace, allowing less than a touchdown per game before getting shredded by Alabama, smothered a Michigan offense built to bully opponents.

The Bulldogs were having none of that.

Dean, the Butkus Award-winning linebacker, diagnosed plays before the snap and chased down ball carriers from sideline to sideline.

Dean said he made note of how heading into this game, for the first time all season, Georgia's defensive dominance seemed to be in doubt.

"We always want to play with a chip on our shoulder," said Dean, who had seven tackles, two for losses, and a forced a fumble.

Massive nose tackle Jordan Davis collapsed the middle of a Michigan offensive line that won the Joe Moore Award as the best in the country.

"That was our plan going in, being a physical, more dominant front," the All-American Davis said.

Cornerback Derion Kendrick, a transfer for Clemson, had two interceptions and was the defensive player of the game.

The Wolverines finished with 88 yards rushing after coming in averaging 223 per game. McNamara was 11 for 19 for 106 yards passing.

Simply, it was no contest and now the Bulldogs will get a shot at redemption against Alabama, trying to win their first national title since 1980.

All that stands in the way is the most accomplished dynasty in the history of college football, and the rival Smart, a longtime Nick Saban assistant at Alabama, has tried to model his program after.

Smart dodged the celebratory Gatorade bath from his players after the game, Smart said he wanted to get a real shower and get to work on catching the team Georgia has been chasing for five years.

(Alabama) got a five, six-hour head start," Smart said. "To be honest with you guys, I'm not interested in celebrating that."

Georgia receiver Adonai Mitchell catches a touchdown pass as Michigan defensive back Vincent Gray looks on during the first half.

Michigan quarterback Cade McNamara is sacked by a swarm of Georgia defenders in the Orange Bowl.

Georgia quarterback Stetson Bennett celebrates during the fourth quarter against Michigan.

Georgia linebacker Nakobe Dean chases down Michigan running back Blake Corum.

Georgia players, along with coach Kirby Smart, lift the Orange Bowl trophy after defeating Michigan.

Georgia fans and players celebrate after clinching a national championship rematch with Alabama.

No.	Name	Pos.	Ht.	Wt.	Year	Hometown
0	Rian Davis	ILB	6-2	230	R-So.	Apopka, Fla. / Wekiva
0	Darnell Washington	TE	6-7	265	So.	Las Vegas, Nev. / Desert Pines
1	Nyland Green	DB	6-1	185	Fr.	Covington, Ga. / Newton
1	George Pickens	WR	6-3	200	Jr.	Hoover, Ala. / Hoover
2	Kendall Milton	RB	6-1	220	So.	Fresno, Calif. / Buchanan
2	Smael Mondon Jr.	LB	6-3	220	Fr.	Dallas, Ga. / Paulding County
3	Kamari Lassiter	DB	6-0	180	Fr.	Savannah, Ga. / Am. Christian Acad.
3	Zamir White	RB	6-0	215	Jr.	Laurinburg, N.C. / Scotland
4	James Cook	RB	5-11	190	Sr.	Miami, Fla. / Miami Central
4	Nolan Smith	OLB	6-3	235	Jr.	Savannah, Ga. / IMG Academy
5	Adonai Mitchell	WR	6-4	190	Fr.	Missouri City, Texas / Cane Ridge
5	Kelee Ringo	DB	6-2	205	R-Fr.	Tacoma, Wash. / Saguaro (Ariz.)
6	Jalen Kimber	DB	6-0	170	R-Fr.	Mansfield, Texas / Timberview
6	Kenny McIntosh	RB	6-1	210	Jr.	Ft. Lauderdale, Fla. / University School
7	Jermaine Burton	WR	6-0	200	So.	Calabasas, Calif. / Calabasas
7	Quay Walker	ILB	6-4	240	Jr.	Cordele, Ga. / Crisp County
8	Dominick Blaylock	WR	6-1	205	R-So.	Marietta, Ga. / Walton
8	MJ Sherman	OLB	6-2	250	So.	Baltimore, Md. / St. John's College
9	Justin Robinson	WR	6-4	220	R-Fr.	McDonough, Ga. / Eagles Landing
9	Ameer Speed	DB	6-3	211	Sr.	Jacksonville, Fla. / Sandalwood
10	Jamon Dumas-Johnson	LB	6-1	235	Fr.	Hyattsville, Md. / St. Frances Academy
10	Kearis Jackson	WR	6-0	200	Jr.	Fort Valley, Ga. / Peach County
11	Derion Kendrick	DB	6-0	190	Sr.	Rock Hill, S.C. / S. Pointe
11	Arian Smith	WR	6-0	185	R-Fr.	Bradley, Fla. / Lakeland
12	Lovasea Carroll	DB	6-1	195	Fr.	Warrenton, Ga. / IMG Academy
12	Brock Vandagriff	QB	6-3	205	Fr.	Bogart, Ga. / Prince Avenue Christian School
13	Stetson Bennett	QB	5-11	190	Sr.	Blackshear, Ga. / Pierce Cty.)
14	David Daniel	DB	6-2	185	Fr.	Woodstock, Ga. / Woodstock
14	Arik Gilbert	WR	6-5	248	So.	Marietta, Ga. / Marietta LSU
14	Jackson Muschamp	QB	6-2	190	R-Fr.	Columbia, S.C. / Hammond School
15	Carson Beck	QB	6-4	215	R-Fr.	Jacksonville, Fla. / Mandarin
15	Trezmen Marshall	ILB	6-1	230	R-So.	Homerville, Ga. / Clinch County
16	Lewis Cine	DB	6-1	200	Jr.	Cedar Hill, Texas / Trinity Christian
17	Nakobe Dean	ILB	6-0	225	Jr.	Horn Lake, Miss. / Horn Lake
17	Jackson Meeks	WR	6-2	205	Fr.	Phenix City, Ala. / Central
18	JT Daniels	QB	6-3	210	Jr.	Irvine, Calif. / Mater Dei
18	Xavian Sorey Jr.	LB	6-3	214	Fr.	Campbellton, Fla. / IMG Academy
19	Adam Anderson	OLB	6-5	230	Sr.	Rome, Ga. / Rome
19	Brock Bowers	TE	6-4	230	Fr.	Napa, Calif. / Napa
20	Sevaughn Clark	RB	6-1	215	R-So.	Dawsonville, Ga. / Dawson County
22	Javon Bullard	DB	5-11	180	Fr.	Milledgeville, Ga. / Baldwin
23	Jaylen Johnson	WR	6-2	192	Jr.	Duluth, Ga. / Peachtree Ridge
23	Tykee Smith	DB	5-10	198	Jr.	Philadelphia, Pa. / Imhotep Institute Charter
24	Matthew Brown	TE	6-2	230	Jr.	Guyton, Ga. / South Effingham
24	Nathan Priestley	QB	6-4	205	R-So.	Los Angeles, Ca. / Loyola
25	Steven Peterson	WR	6-2	214	Jr.	Kennesaw, Ga. / Harrison
26	Jehlen Cannady	DB	6-0	176	R-Fr.	Macon, Ga. / Westside
26	Collin Drake	QB	6-1	195	Fr.	Ennis, Texas / Ennis
29	Christopher Smith	DB	5-11	190	Sr.	Atlanta, Ga. / Hapeville Charter
31	William Poole	DB	6-0	190	Sr.	Atlanta, Ga. / Hapeville Charter
32	Chaz Chambliss	LB	6-2	250	Fr.	Carrollton, Ga. / Carrollton
32	Cash Jones	RB	6-0	182	Fr.	Brock, Texas / Brock
33	Robert Beal Jr.	OLB	6-4	255	Jr.	Duluth, Ga. / Peachtree Ridge
33	Daijun Edwards	RB	5-10	201	So.	Norman Park, Ga. / Colquitt County
35	John Staton IV	LB	6-1	225	Gr.	Atlanta, Ga. / The Lovett School
36	Latavious Brini	DB	6-2	210	Sr.	Miami Gardens, Fla. / Mater Academy Charter
36	Garrett Jones	RB	6-0	203	Jr.	Albany, Ga. / Deerfield-Windsor
37	Drew Southern	DB	5-11	180	Fr.	Cumming, Ga. / West Forsyth
37	Woody Waters	WR	5-8	160	R-Fr.	Newnan, Ga. / Newnan
38	Patrick Taylor	DB	6-0	175	R-Fr.	Johns Creek, Ga. / Johns Creek
39	Brady Tindall	WR	5-10	192	Sr.	Atlanta, Ga. / The Lovett School
41	Channing Tindall	ILB	6-2	230	Sr.	Columbia, S.C. / Spring Valley
42	Graham Collins	ILB	6-2	215	R-Fr.	Atlanta, Ga. / Holy Innocents Episcopal School
43	Chase Harof	TE	6-2	250	Sr.	Roswell, Ga. / Blessed Trinity
43	Matthew Helow	DB	5-11	175	Fr.	Jacksonville, Fla. / (Bishop Kenny)
44	Michael Hagerty	TE	6-4	225	R-So.	Hinesville, Ga. / Bradwell Institute
44	Travon Walker	DL	6-5	275	Jr.	Thomaston, Ga. / Upson-Lee
45	Kurt Knisely	RB	6-0	200	R-Fr.	Watkinsville, Ga. / Athens Academy
45	Bill Norton	DL	6-6	300	R-So.	Memphis, Tenn. / Christian Brothers
46	Payton Bowles	DB	5-10	170	R-Fr.	Athens, Ga. / Athens Academy
47	Dan Jackson	DB	6-1	190	R-So.	Gainesville, Ga. / North Hall
47	Payne Walker	SN	6-2	249	Jr.	Suwanee, Ga. / North Gwinnett
48	Wesley Potter	DB	6-3	205	Jr.	Canton, Ga. / Sequoyah
49	Gleaton Jones	RB	6-1	200	Fr.	Albany, Ga. / Deerfield-Windsor
50	Warren Ericson	OL	6-4	305	Jr.	Suwanee, Ga. / North Gwinnett
51	Tate Ratledge	OL	6-6	320	R-Fr.	Rome, Ga. / Darlington School
52	Cameron Kinnie	OL	6-3	300	Fr.	Suwanee, Ga. / Collins Hill
53	Dylan Fairchild	OL	6-5	300	Fr.	Cumming, Ga. / West Forsyth HS
54	Cade Brock	ILB	6-0	250	R-Fr.	Subligna, Ga. / Darlington
54	Justin Shaffer	OL	6-4	330	Sr.	Ellenwood, Ga. / Cedar Grove
55	Marlin Dean	DL	6-5	275	Fr.	Bowman, Ga. / IMG Academy
55	Jared Wilson	OL	6-3	330	Fr.	Winston-Salem, N.C. / West Forsyth HS
56	Micah Morris	OL	6-6	330	Fr.	Kingsland, Ga. / Camden County
56	William Mote	SN	6-2	230	R-So.	Hoover, Ala. / Spain Park
57	Luke Collins	OLB	6-2	245	Fr.	Birmingham, Ala. / Birmingham Prep
58	Austin Blaske	OL	6-5	310	R-Fr.	Faulkville, Ga. / South Effingham
59	Broderick Jones	OL	6-4	315	R-Fr.	Lithonia, Ga. / Lithonia
60	Clay Webb	OL	6-3	290	R-So.	Oxford, Ala. / Oxford
61	Blake Watson	OL	6-6	300	Jr.	Roswell, Ga. / Milton
63	Sedrick Van Pran	OL	6-4	310	R-Fr.	New Orleans, La. / Warren Easton
65	Amarius Mims	OL	6-7	330	Fr.	Cochran, Ga. / Bleckley County
66	Jonathan Washburn	SN	6-2	230	Fr.	Ringgold, Ga. / Heritage
67	John Ferguson	OL	6-5	270	Fr.	Athens, Ga. / Athens Academy
68	Chris Brown	OL	6-5	300	R-Fr.	Savannah, Ga. / Islands
69	Jamaree Salyer	OL	6-4	325	Sr.	Atlanta, Ga. / Pace Academy
70	Warren McClendon	OL	6-4	300	R-So.	Brunswick, Ga. / Brunswick
73	Xavier Truss	OL	6-7	330	R-So.	West Warwick, R.I. / Bishop Hendricken
75	Owen Condon	OL	6-7	310	Jr.	Oklahoma City, Okla. / Bishop McGuinness
76	Miles Johnson	OL	6-5	320	R-Fr.	Blue Ridge, Ga. / Fannin County
77	Devin Willock	OL	6-7	335	R-Fr.	New Milford, N.J. / Paramus Catholic
78	Chad Lindberg	OL	6-6	325	Fr.	League City, Texas / Clear Creek
78	Nazir Stackhouse	DL	6-3	320	So.	Stone Mountain, Ga. / Columbia
79	Weston Wallace	OL	6-3	320	R-Fr.	Eatonton, Ga. / Gatewood School
80	Brett Seither	TE	6-5	228	R-So.	Clearwater, Fla. / Clearwater Central Catholic
81	Marcus Rosemy-Jacksaint	WR	6-2	195	So.	Pompano Beach, Fla. / St. Thomas Aquinas
82	Logan Johnson	WR	5-6	155	Fr.	Bogart, Ga. / Prince Avenue Christian School
84	Ladd McConkey	WR	6-0	185	R-Fr.	Chatsworth, Ga. / North Murray
85	Drew Sheehan	TE	6-2	215	R-So.	Woodstock, Ga. / Woodstock
86	John FitzPatrick	TE	6-7	250	Jr.	Atlanta, Ga. / Marist School
87	Mekhi Mews	WR	5-8	170	Fr.	Grayson, Ga. / Central Gwinnett
88	Jalen Carter	DL	6-3	310	So.	Apopka, Fla. / Apopka
88	Ryland Goede	TE	6-6	240	R-So.	Kennesaw, Ga. / Kennesaw Mountain
89	Malcolm Brown	DL	6-0	270	Fr.	Guyton, Ga. / South Effingham
89	Braxton Hicks	WR	6-2	195	R-Fr.	Tiger, Ga. / Rabun County
90	Jake Camarda	PK/P	6-2	180	Sr.	Norcross, Ga. / Norcross
90	Tramel Walthour	DL	6-3	280	Jr.	Hinesville, Ga. / Liberty County
91	Tymon Mitchell	DL	6-3	300	R-So.	Nashville, Tenn. / Franklin Road Academy
92	Julian Rochester	DL	6-5	300	Sr.	Mableton, Ga. / McEachern
93	Tyrion Ingram-Dawkins	DL	6-5	300	Fr.	Gaffney, S.C. / Gaffney
94	Jonathan Jefferson	DL	6-3	295	Fr.	Douglasville, Ga. / Douglas County
95	Noah Chumley	P	6-3	185	R-So.	Savannah, Ga. / Savannah Christian
95	Devonte Wyatt	DL	6-3	315	Sr.	Decatur, Ga. / Towers
96	Zion Logue	DL	6-5	295	R-So.	Lebanon, Tenn. / Lebanon
96	Jack Podlesny	PK	6-1	180	Jr.	St. Simons Island, Ga. / Glynn Academy
97	Warren Brinson	DT	6-4	305	So.	Savannah, Ga. / IMG Academy
97	Matthew Sumlin	PK/P	5-11	170	R-Fr.	Smyrna, Ga. / Whitefield Academy
98	Noah Jones	P	6-0	165	Fr.	Cairo, Ga. / Cairo
98	Tyler Malakius	DL	6-3	280	R-So.	Byron, Ga. / Westfield
99	Jordan Davis	DL	6-6	340	Sr.	Charlotte, N.C. / Mallard Creek
99	Jared Zirkel	PK	6-3	185	R-Fr.	Kerrville, Texas / Tivy